Dear Little One, God Planned You

Written and Illustrated

by

Josie Syverson

ISBN 978-1-960903-35-8 (Digital)

ISBN 978-1-960903-36-5 (Paperback)

ISBN 978-1-960903-88-4 (Hardcover)

Copyright © 2023 Josie Syverson

All Rights Reserved. No part of this publication may be reproduced, distributed, or transmitted in any form or by any means, including photocopying, recording, or other electronic or mechanical methods without the prior written permission of the publisher. For permission requests, solicit the publisher via the address below.

Publify Publishing

1412 W. Ave B

Lampasas, TX 76550

publifypublishing@gmail.com

"For you created my inmost being; you knit me together in my mother's womb. I praise you because I am fearfully and wonderfully made; your works are wonderful; I know that full well. My frame was not hidden from you when I was made in the secret place, when I was woven together in the depths of the earth. Your eyes saw my unformed body; all the days ordained for me were written in your book before one of them came to be."

Psalm 139:13–16, NIV

My dear Little One,

When I found out that you were in my tummy, it surprised me! But you did not surprise God! God knew you were there even before I did. In fact, God is the One who put you there. Before the beginning of time, God was planning *you*! And God loved you, even before He put you in my tummy!

God planned whether you would be a precious boy or girl. He planned what color of skin, eyes, and hair would be best for you; whether you would be tall or short; whether you would be best with or without freckles.

God planned your personality, too. I can't wait to see whether God has planned for you to be shy or outgoing, to be talkative or quiet.

Then God planned when and where you should live. Because God was planning you to be such a special person, He wanted to be sure to send you at just the right time to just the right house in just the right town and in just the right country. God could have put you anywhere in the whole world, but He chose to place you right here and right now—right in my tummy! How blessed I am!

And Little One, God knows exactly how your life will be and exactly how long you will live. He knows what will make you happy and what will make you sad, and He wants you to let Him be there for you through it all! He knows what your favorite subject in school will be, what your favorite summer activity will be, who your friends will be, and even if or to whom you will get married.

God's got an amazing life planned out for you, Little One. And He's making you to be one amazing person! There is a spot in this world that only you can fill, and God wants you to fill it with love. You see, God is putting you here and now because He has given you a job: to love God and love people in a way no one else can! And when you love God and people in your special, God-given way, that makes God happy, and you will be bringing Him glory!

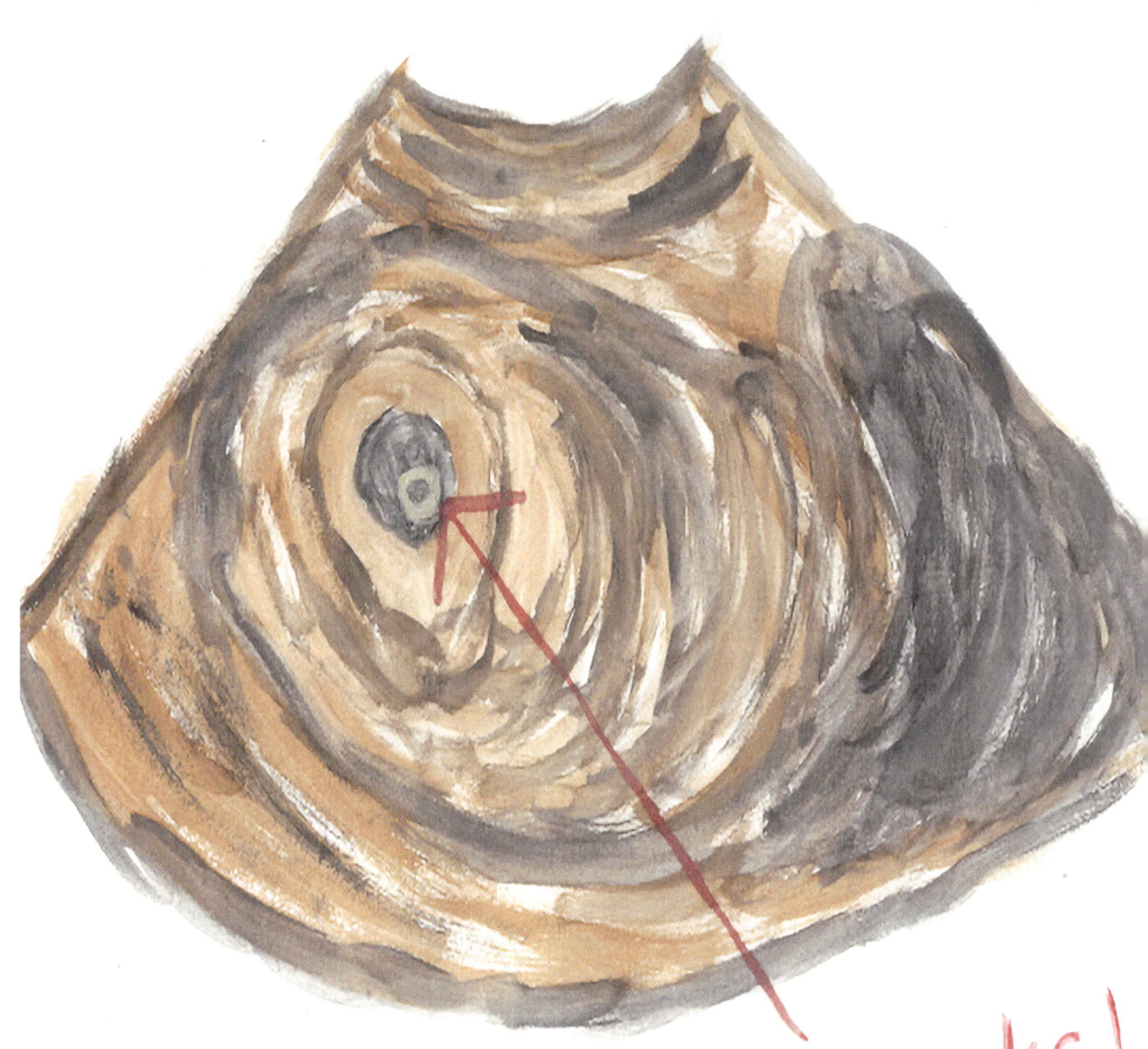

Now, Little One, let me tell you how God has been making you in my tummy! First, you began so, so tiny. But even when you were that teeny-tiny, God saw you as a very special person, and He loved you! Already, God had put everything in you that would give you your own special personality and that would make you grow as that special young man or young woman that He planned for you to be.

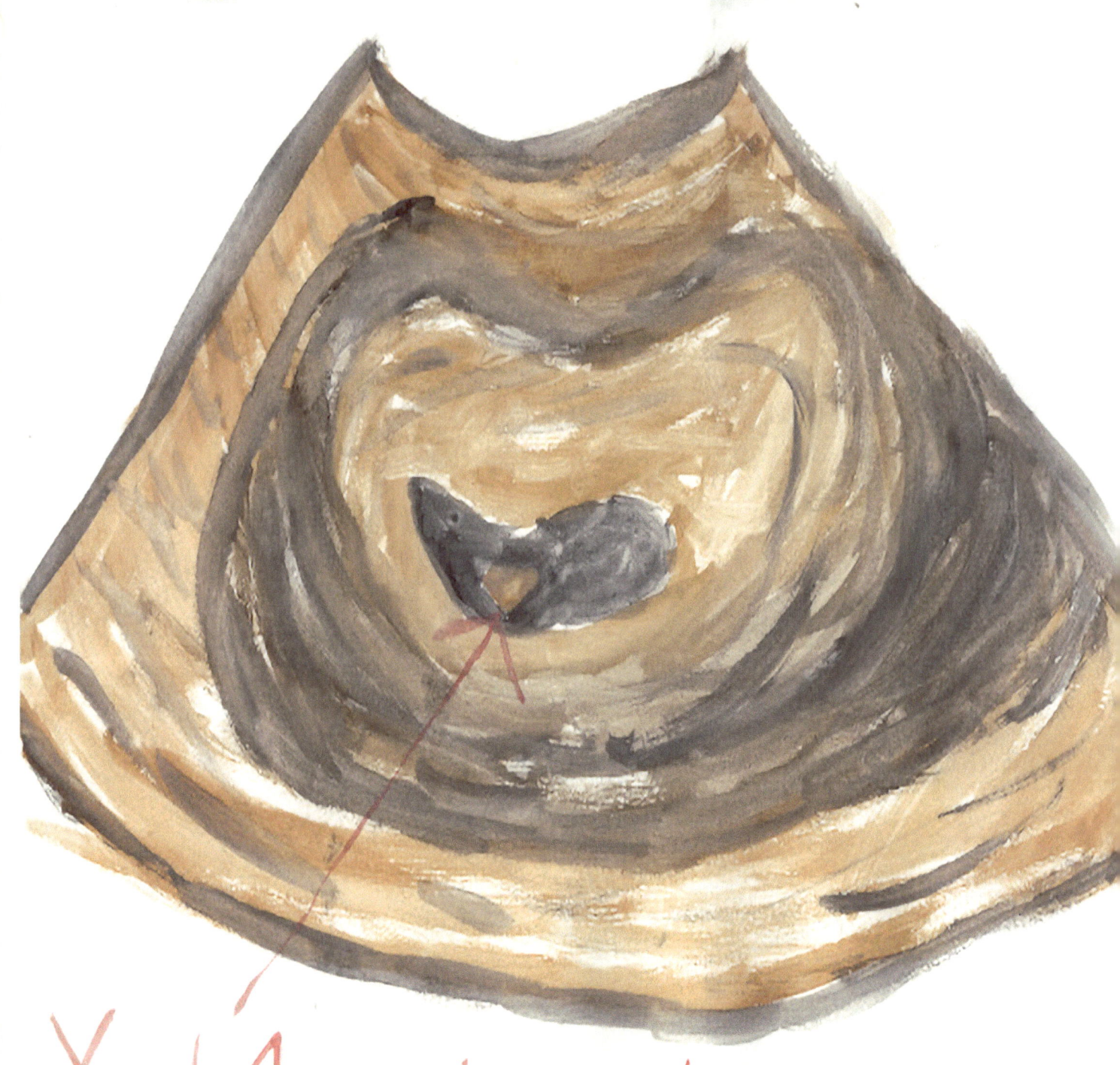

God began growing and changing you immediately! When you were seventeen days old, God was making your circulatory system, and your heart began its lifelong beating when you were twenty-one days. Your digestive system was also being formed while you were just twenty-one days old. When you were four weeks old, God formed your detailed system of blood vessels. He also made your respiratory system, but your lungs' use would be saved for your first of many breaths outside of my body. You were shaped sort of like a tadpole then and were smaller than a grain of rice. But no matter how small you were, you were—and are—my precious baby!

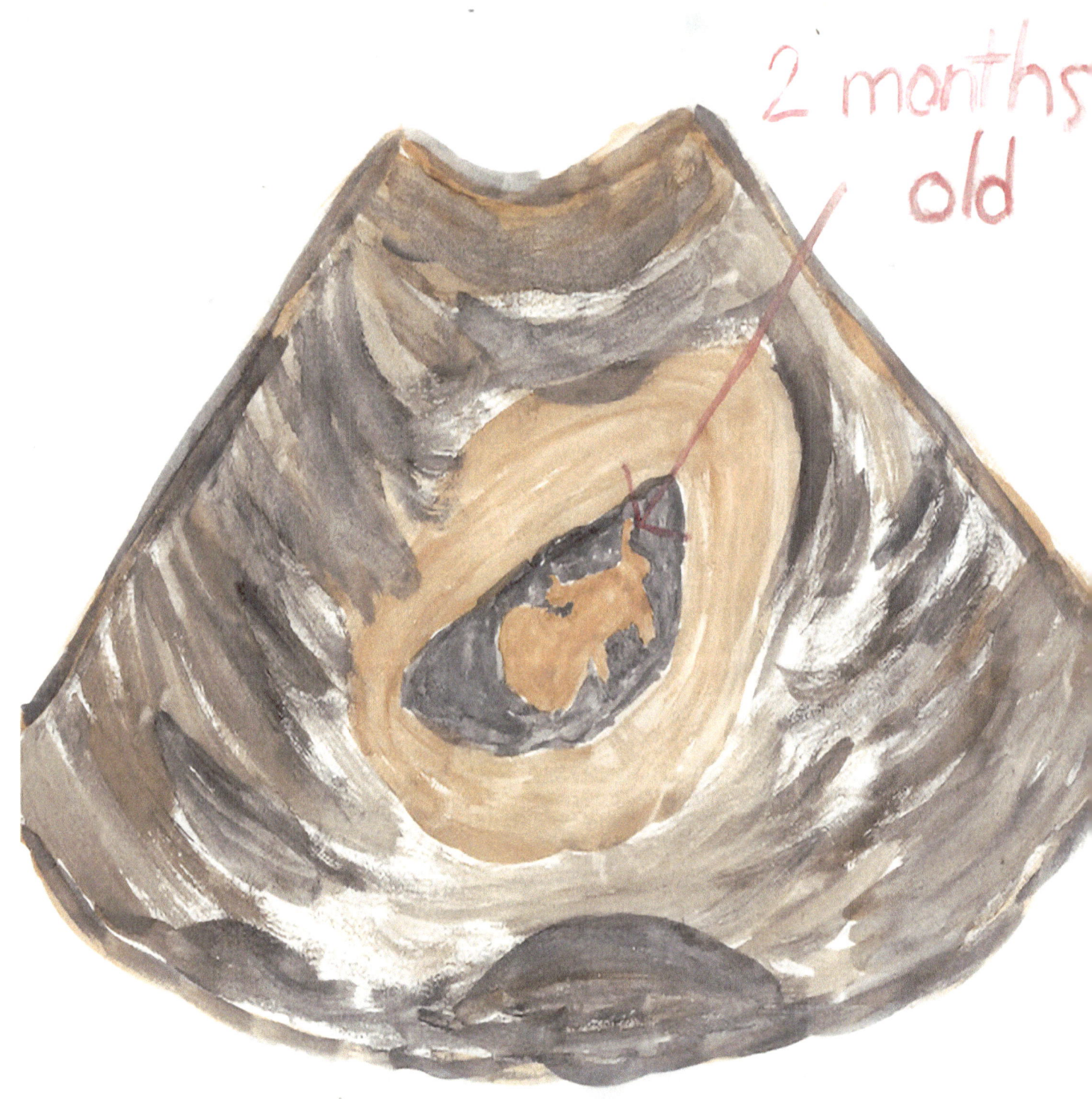

2 months old

At the age of five weeks, your skeleton was taking shape. By six weeks, your brain was beginning to send messages out to control your nervous system; your kidneys began filtering your blood, and your stomach began producing digestive juices. When you were seven weeks old, you began responding to touch. At eight weeks, all your organs were formed; some of your cartilage began being replaced by bone, a process that will last until you reach the age of twenty-five years. Your face was receiving its beautiful features, and your fingers and toes were starting to take shape. You were starting to take on your baby form! With your legs tucked up, you were now one and one-fourth inches long and weighed about one-third of an ounce.

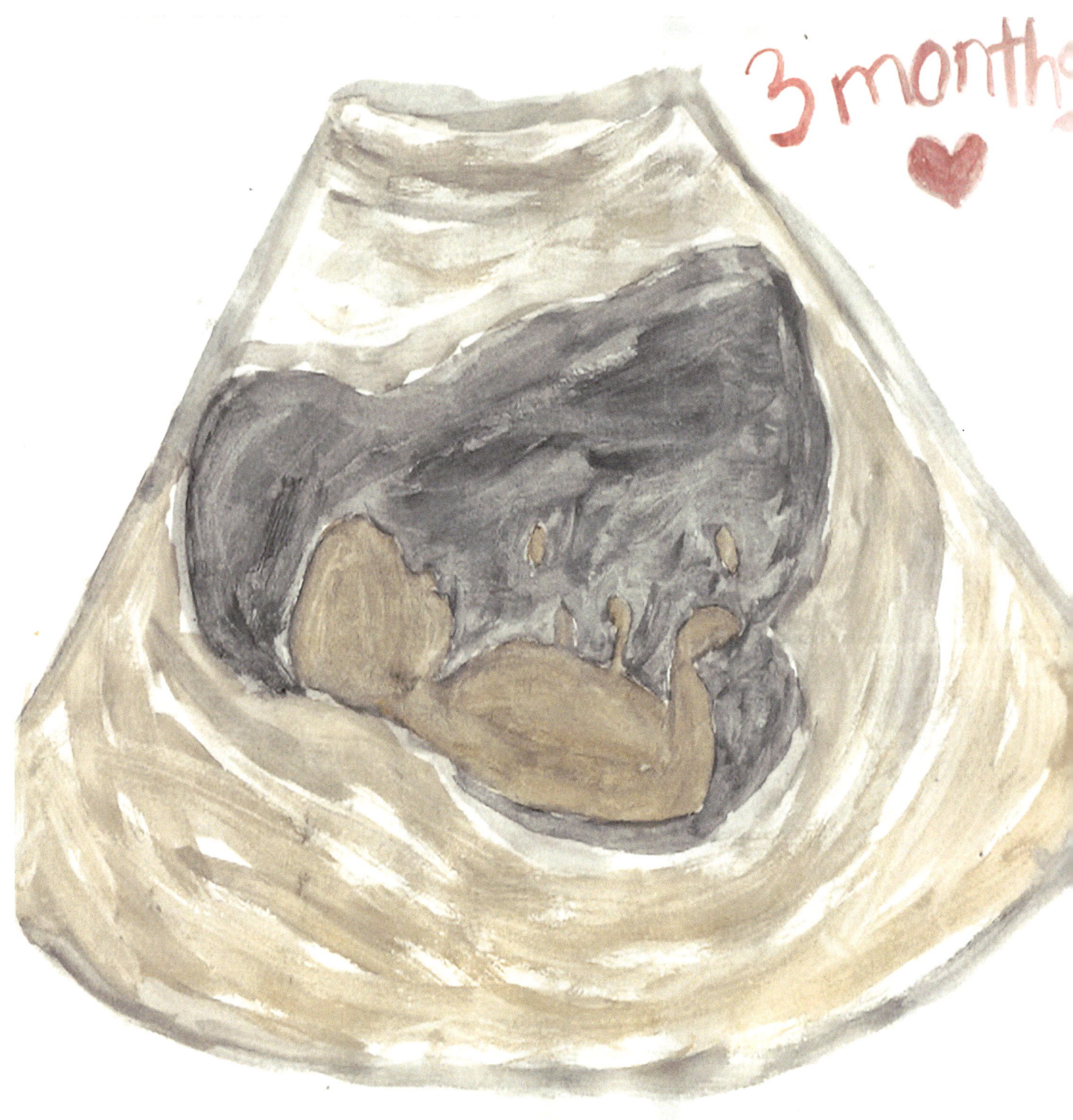

When you reached the age of ten weeks, you began moving your muscles, and your kidneys began working full time. By twelve weeks, your brain was fully formed, and your circulatory and urinary systems began working. You began responding to your environment and would now be able to feel pain if it were inflicted. By the end of your third month of age, every detail of the basic structures of your little being was developed! You were then three inches long, half of an ounce in weight, and oh! so beautiful!

Beautiful you! 4 months!

During your fourth month of age, you began developing reflexes that allowed you to both suck and swallow. Your tooth buds appeared, and your fingers and toes grew and became beautifully defined. You then reached the length of four inches.

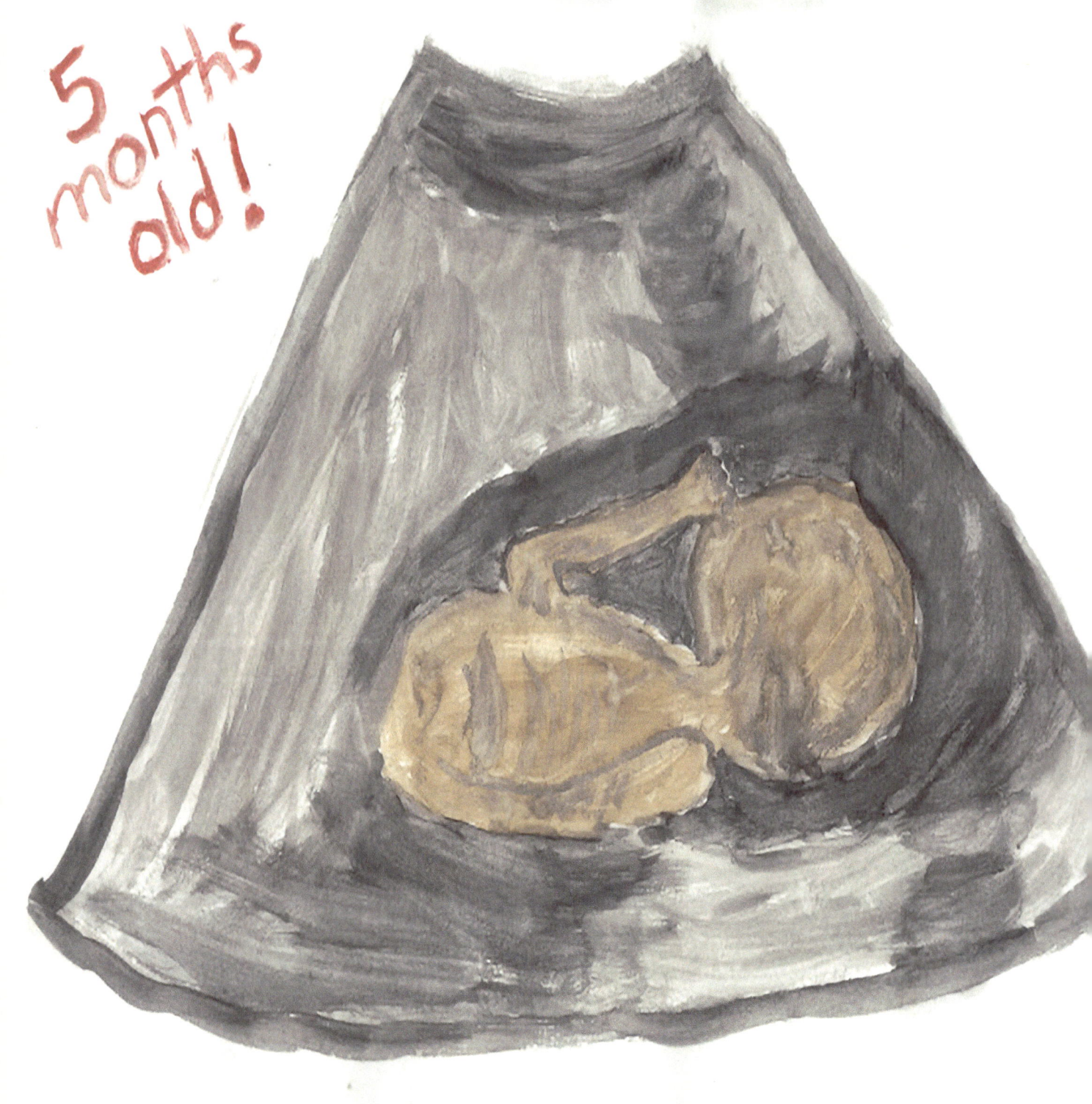

By the end of your fifth month, you were about nine inches long. Hair, then, grew on your head and eyebrows, and white hair grew in as your eyelashes. Then you began to move! I will never forget the first time I saw your body turn, or felt you kick! Oh, I fell in love with you every day!

6 months ♥

In your sixth month, your skin became thin and shiny, and your finger and toe prints became visible. And then you opened your eyes. You were growing so fast that you quickly grew to thirteen inches in length and one and three-fourths pounds in weight.

you at 7 months.

When you were seven months, you started collecting some fat on yourself! You were then able to hiccup, cry, suck your thumb, taste sweet or sour, and respond to light or sound. I've made sure to talk to you a lot, haven't I? You now weighed about three pounds. As you got bigger and bigger and took up more and more room inside of me, you became a little less active and were more still in my tummy.

8 months old

By the end of your eighth month, the only thing left to develop was your lungs. You had now reached eighteen inches in length and weighed five pounds.

You now— at 9 months

And that brings us up to now! By now your lungs are well developed, and you are growing more and more in length and weight.

All these months—from your very tiny beginning and beyond—God has been fearfully and wonderfully creating you! He has been planning and fashioning you in awe and reverence in the most wonderful, extraordinary, and loving way! God has been creating you in His glorious image! And all of this—God's image and awe and wonder—has been wrapped up in you since your very beginning, and since the very beginning when God was first thinking of you! *You are so special!* And you are being put here for a very special purpose!

So, dear Little One, planned and purposed by your amazing Creator God, until I get to see you face-to-face, I want you to remember several things. Remember that you were planned by an Almighty and loving God, that neither you nor any detail of you is an accident. Remember that God loves you more than you will ever know, and that you will glorify Him and fulfill your purpose when you love Him and others in your special, God-given way. Last of all, remember that I always have and always will love you, my Little One!

Love,
Your Momma

Dear You,

You are not an accident. Your life is not a mistake. Both you and your life were planned by God. (If you have had troubles and hardships in your life, understand that God did not plan harm for you, but allows that which will bring Him glory, draw you close to Himself, and refine you out of His great love for you.) Your gender, skin color, place of residence, etc. are not mistakes but details planned by an Amazing God who loves you infinitely, has an amazing plan for your life here on earth, and ultimately wants to spend eternity with you! You are a masterpiece created fearfully and wonderfully in God's image! And not just you, but every person of every nation and tongue as well!

Think of what this means for a minute: the implications this fact has. If God has made you, then no one has the right to take your life but God. If God has made me, then no one has the right to take my life but God. If God has planned and created in His image babies, then from conception, they are His, and no one has the right to take their lives but Him. If God has made the disabled and has a purpose and abounding love for them, they are His, and no one has the right to decide that their lives are worthless and so deprive them of life. If God has made the elderly and given them the blessing of many years of life in which they can choose to serve and love Him and people, no one has the right to "mercifully" end their days but

God Himself.

Abortion . . . euthanasia . . . it's all murder. God has said, "And from each human being, too, I will demand an accounting for the life of another human being" *(Genesis 9:5, NIV).*

God has also said, "I am the Alpha and the Omega, the Beginning and the End. To the thirsty I will give water without cost from the spring of the water of life. Those who are victorious will inherit all this, and I will be their God and they will be my children. But the cowardly, the unbelieving, the vile, the murderers, the sexually immoral, those who practice magic arts, the idolaters and all liars—they will be consigned to the fiery lake of burning sulfur. This is the second death" *(Revelation 21:6–8, NIV).*

God gives life. Only God has the right to take life. We must stand with God in loving opposition to murder—in all its forms—and stand for and support the sanctity of life.

You are planned by God, as is everyone. Support the lives of the unborn and of the elderly and the disabled. God has a planned purpose for each individual. To oppose that is to stand in danger of the fires of Hell.

Choose life!

I pray that this story will be a blessing to all hearts—no matter their age!

The Roman Road[1]

Romans 3:23—"For all have sinned and fall short of the glory of God."

Romans 5:8—"But God demonstrates his own love for us in this: While we were still sinners, Christ died for us."

Romans 6:23—"For the wages of sin is death, but the gift of God is eternal life in Christ Jesus our Lord."

Romans 8:1—"Therefore, there is now no condemnation for those who are in Christ Jesus."

Romans 10:9—"If you declare with your mouth, 'Jesus is Lord,' and believe in your heart that God raised him from the dead, you will be saved."

---

[1] All quotations are from the NIV.

You were planned and created by a loving and just God. But you are a sinner. You deserve Hell, as do I. But Jesus wants to have a relationship with you here on earth, and He wants to spend an eternity with you in Heaven. So, Jesus died for you on the cross and then rose from the dead. Today He is preparing a place for you in Heaven if you will confess your sins and believe that He is Lord. All you have to do is trust Him to save you, and He will. Ask Him to fill you with love for Him and other people, and then share Jesus with everyone (by your love, they will know that you follow Jesus).

If you have asked Jesus to save you, find a Bible-believing church where you can learn more about Jesus and get to know other Christians. Also, get a Bible (I would recommend NIV) and begin to read. Start in the book of John and read a little every day.

Jesus bless you!

References

I. Eisenberg, Arene, Heidi E. Murkoff, and Sandee E. Hathaway. *What to Expect when You're Expecting.* 2nd ed. New York: Workman Publishing Company, 1994.

II. Parker, Gregory, Keith Graham, Delores Shimmin, and George Thompson. *Biology: God's Living Creation.* 2nd ed. Pensacola, FL: A Beka Books, 1997.

AUTHOR BIO

Josie Syverson lives in Southeast Minnesota. She grew up in a family of eleven where she was blessed with a home-education and the foundation for an ongoing relationship with Jesus Christ.

Since a young age, Josie dreamed of being a writer; she is so thankful to Jesus for making that dream now come true!

www.ingramcontent.com/pod-product-compliance
Lightning Source LLC
Chambersburg PA
CBHW041414010526
44107CB00016B/1162